A REAL LIFE FAIRY TALE

JACKIE KENNEDY

A REAL LIFE FAIRY TALE

JACKIE
KENNEDY

Written by Emberli Pridham

Illustrated by Danilo Cerovic

gatekeeper press™
TAMPA, FLORIDA

A Real Life Fairy Tale Jackie Kennedy

Published by Gatekeeper Press

7853 Gunn Hwy., Suite 209
Tampa, FL 33626

www.GatekeeperPress.com

Library of Congress Control Number: 2023952146

ISBN (hardcover): 9781662947063

ISBN (paperback): 9781662947070

eISBN: 9781662947087

This book is dedicated to my wonderful children who inspire me every day.

– Emberli Pridham

Once there was a girl named Jacqueline Bouvier

   with beautiful brown hair and brown eyes.

From an early age, she loved to ride horses,

   and, in tournaments, she'd often win first prize!

Jackie lived in Southampton and New York City,

with her mother, her sister and dad.

Her father encouraged her independence and vivacity

and said she was "the most beautiful daughter a man ever had."

*L*ittle Jackie loved to read and take ballet lessons.

For foreign languages, she had quite an ear.

In high school, she graduated near the top of her class

and was declared "debutante of the year."

*J*ackie joined many clubs at Vassar College,

the art club, drama club, and newspaper too.

She studied French Literature at the Sorbonne in Paris

and got her degree at George Washington U.

After college, Jackie was an "Inspiring Camera Girl"

at the Washington Times-Herald newspaper.

But covering Queen Elizabeth's coronation was an experience destined to shape her.

In Washington, Jackie met a U.S. Senator

named John Fitzgerald Kennedy.

In just a few months, they fell in love,

and marriage was their destiny!

In Newport, Rhode Island, they held their wedding

with 1,200 distinguished guests attending.

LIFE

A STAGGERING JOB OF REORGANIZATION
NEIL McELROY'S PENTAGON
HOW A FAMILY GUIDES ITS CHILDREN
TO GET A KICK OUT OF LEARNING

JACQUELINE, CAROLINE
AND JACK KENNEDY

APRIL 21, 1958   25 CENTS

*T*he couple soon welcomed baby Caroline,

and people were curious, Jackie discovered.

When Jackie's husband ran for President,

Life magazine put their family on the cover!

The CARLYLE

While campaigning for her husband, John,

Jackie was admired for her sense of style.

She wore clothes by Chanel, and, when in New York,

she loved staying at the Hotel Carlyle.

When John Kennedy was elected President,

he and Jackie were well-loved, it was clear.

Two weeks later, baby John Jr. was born, and

Jackie was named Time magazine's Woman of the Year.

America loved watching Caroline and John Jr.

at birthday parties when they played and rode ponies.

Vice President Johnson even gave Caroline a gift:

a little pony named Macaroni!

*J*ackie tastefully restored the White House and the Rose Garden beautifully. She even won a special Emmy Award when she gave a White House tour on TV.

The White House showcased many performers

like poet Robert Frost and conductor Leonard Bernstein.

The Metropolitan Opera, the American Ballet Theater,

and Jackie's "Concerts for Young People" also shined.

*J*ackie traveled to many foreign countries,

speaking French, Spanish, and Italian.

The President of Pakistan, Ayub Khan,

gave her Sardar, a beautiful stallion.

The French gave Jackie the French Legion of Honor

because of her love of French culture and history.

She was truly admired the world over,

and the reason wasn't a mystery.

When President Kennedy was assassinated,

it was a tragic day for the nation.

But Jackie, Caroline, and John Jr. stayed strong,

earning the family much admiration.

Though no longer in the White House,

Jackie's schedule was still quite demanding.

She became a Goodwill Ambassador for the United Nations

to promote cross-cultural awareness and understanding.

*J*ackie moved to New York City to add "book editor" to her growing resume.

While continuing to be a respected diplomat, she worked for Viking Press and Doubleday.

Jackie found that she still had a passion
for culture and historic preservation.
She worked long and hard to save
New York's Grand Central Station.

$\mathcal{B}$oth of Jackie's childen grew up
to be successful and appreciated.
Caroline became a U.S. Ambassador,
and John Jr. edited George, a magazine
he created.

*J*ackie Kennedy lived a remarkable life

as a diplomat, art and book lover, and mother.

She often said, "There are many ways

to enlarge your child's world.

And the love of books is the best of all."

The End

Emberli Pridham grew up in Dallas, Texas, inspired by her grandmother, an author, and a wonderful library of books. She, along with her husband, David, are the co-authors of the Amazon best-selling STEM book series, *If Not You, Then Who?*, which aims to teach children about the inventions and patents in everyday life, inspiring and empowering them to imagine and create their own.

Emberli is currently writing the next two books about inspiring and influential people for the *Real Life Fairy Tale series*. She also spends her time taking care of her beautiful family and is extensively involved in philanthropic work on behalf of the Hasbro Children's Hospital, Dallas Museum of Art, Dallas Symphony, Elton John AIDS Foundation, and American Cancer Society, among other charities.

The Pridhams live and split their time between Texas and Rhode Island with their three ever-curious children, Brooke, Noah, and Graham.

For more information, visit areallifefairytalebooks.com
Follow on Instagram @reallifefairytaleseries

Milton Keynes UK
Ingram Content Group UK Ltd.
UKHW051205080824
446708UK00036B/502